Federal Advisory Committee on Juvenile Justice

2013 Recommendations to the President, Congress, and OJJDP Administrator

July 2014

Mr. Robert L. Listenbee
Administrator
Office of Juvenile Justice and Delinquency Prevention
Office of Justice Programs
U.S. Department of Justice
Washington, DC 20531

Dear Mr. Listenbee,

As you know, the Federal Advisory Committee on Juvenile Justice (FACJJ) is a consultative body established by the Juvenile Justice and Delinquency Prevention Act (section 223) and supported by the Office of Juvenile Justice and Delinquency Prevention (OJJDP) within the U.S. Department of Justice, Office of Justice Programs. The charter for the FACJJ provides that—

> *The FACJJ will review federal policies regarding juvenile justice and delinquency prevention; advise the Administrator with respect to particular functions or aspects of the work of the Office; advise the President and Congress with regard to the operation of the Office and federal legislation pertaining to juvenile justice and delinquency prevention; and provide advice on any other matters as requested by the Administrator.*

After reconfiguring the membership in late 2011, the FACJJ established subcommittees to develop recommendations to the full committee that address four areas of major concern to the juvenile justice community. On behalf of the FACJJ, we are pleased to convey to you, through this report, the recommendations adopted by the FACJJ for your consideration as you work on significant issues that impact the future of youth and our communities. We urge you to forward these recommendations to the Attorney General, the President, and the Congress as appropriate.

We clearly recognize the complexity and scope of issues and challenges facing OJJDP and the states, and we understand that the recommendations in this report represent only a portion of the many issues that we know concern you, our members, the State Advisory Groups, and juvenile justice practitioners throughout the country. The report itself provides some of the context and scope of what went into the work of the various subcommittees and a number of specific recommendations in each of the four areas of interest. We stand ready to discuss them further with you as needed to help guide OJJDP's efforts.

On behalf of our members, we want to recognize and extend our appreciation to all OJJDP staff who provided assistance to us throughout this process. We look forward to continued dialogue and opportunities to provide input as we work together to build and support a juvenile justice system that is more effective at preventing youth crime, responding to the needs of victims and our communities that are impacted by youth crime, and providing fair and effective responses to youth and families who are involved in the juvenile justice system.

Sincerely,

Reggie Robinson   Robin Lubitz
Chair   Vice Chair

Federal Advisory Committee on Juvenile Justice

PRIMARY MEMBERS*

Dalene Dutton
Executive Director
Five Town Communities That Care
Maine

Tony Jones
Chief of Police
Gainesville Police Department
Florida

ViEve Martin Kohrs
Director of Resource Development
Calcasieu Parish Office of Juvenile
    Justice Services
Louisiana

Kenya Shantel Lee
Founder/CEO
Parents With Power
Maryland
(Alternate member who became primary member
after Robert L. Listenbee's resignation from FACJJ)

Raquel Montoya-Lewis
Chief Judge
Nooksack Indian Tribe and the
    Upper Skagit Indian Tribe
Washington State

Robert L. Listenbee
Chief
Defender Association of Philadelphia
Pennsylvania
(Resigned from FACJJ prior to assuming role of
OJJDP Administrator in March 2013)

Robin L. Lubitz, Vice-Chair (2011–13)
Director of Juvenile Justice Services (retired)
Arizona Juvenile Justice Commission
Arizona

Jim Moeser
Deputy Director
Wisconsin Council on Children and Families
Wisconsin

Claudio Martin Kotomor Norita
Commissioner of Public Safety (retired)
Commonwealth of the Northern
    Mariana Islands

Christine Perra Rapillo
Director of Delinquency Defense
    and Child Protection
Connecticut Office of Chief Public Defender
Connecticut

Haley Rae Reimbold
Graduate Student
Columbia University
New York

Reginald L. Robinson, Chair (2011–13)
Professor of Law and Director
Center for Law and Government
Washburn University School of Law
Kansas

John B. Roe IV
Judge
15th Judicial Circuit Court, Ogle County
Illinois
(Assumed alternate role in October 2013)

Symone D. Sanders
Graduate
Creighton University
Nebraska

Dean R. Williams
Juvenile Justice Superintendent (former)
State of Alaska

*All FACJJ members are representative members of State Advisory Groups throughout the nation. For additional information regarding the FACJJ, including current members and their terms, visit the FACJJ Web site at www.facjj.org.

ALTERNATE MEMBERS*

Aileen Jo Artero
Graduate Student
University of Guam
Guam, Mariana Islands

Pat S. Berckman
Clinical Social Worker
Salt Lake County
Utah

Richard Broderick
Superintendent (retired)
Northeastern Local School District
Ohio

Susan Colling
Coordinator/Management Analyst
Colorado State Judicial Department
Colorado

Joseph Diament
Director
Division of Community Corrections
New Hampshire Department of Corrections
New Hampshire

Martha Doyle
Project Manager/Government Affairs
Cambia Health Solutions
Oregon

William H. Feyerherm
Professor of Criminology and
    Criminal Justice
Portland State University
Oregon

Sarah McBride
President, Student Government (former)
Graduate
American University
Delaware

Liz Mueller
Tribal Council Vice Chair/Government Liaison
Jamestown S'Klallam Tribal Council
Washington State

Maria Estela Quintanilla
Crime Stoppers, Webb County
Sheriff's Office Consultant
Texas

Pili J. Robinson
Director of Consulting Services
Missouri Youth Services Institute
Missouri

George W. Timberlake
Chief Judge (retired)
Second Judicial Circuit in
    Southeastern Illinois
Illinois
(Assumed primary role in October 2013)

Linda Whittington
Representative
Mississippi House District 34
Mississippi

*All FACJJ members are representative members of State Advisory Groups throughout the nation. For additional information regarding the FACJJ, including current members and their terms, visit the FACJJ Web site at www.facjj.org.

Contents

Executive Summary

In its role as advisor to the President, the Congress, and the Office of Juvenile Justice and Delinquency Prevention (OJJDP) on juvenile justice issues, the Federal Advisory Committee on Juvenile Justice (FACJJ) established subcommittees to develop recommendations for consideration by the full FACJJ that address four areas of major concern to the juvenile justice community.

The Evidence-Based Youth Justice Practices Subcommittee's recommendations relate to the study, dissemination, and effective implementation of youth justice-focused programs. The subcommittee looked at the need for evidence-based programs and evidence-based practices, referring to both as EBPs, and the need to bridge the gap between research and practice. The subcommittee stressed that more needs to be done to integrate positive youth development outcomes into EBP work along with reducing negative behaviors. The subcommittee encourages the integration of EBPs into the larger justice framework that views youth, the community, and those affected by crime as equally important customers of the juvenile justice system. The FACJJ recommends that OJJDP take a leadership role in assessing strategies for implementing EBPs systemwide, promoting the development of new practice strategies and resources, emphasizing the need to implement practices and programs based on research about what works, collaborating with other agencies and organizations that work with and support youth and families, and supporting EBPs that can reduce racial disparities in the juvenile justice system.

The Youth Engagement Subcommittee, composed of four young adults who are State Advisory Group and FACJJ youth members, focused on youth voice and engagement in the juvenile justice system and on involving youth with current or prior juvenile justice system experience in shaping the policies and practices of this system at the federal, state, and local levels. The subcommittee noted that involving youth as partners can help transform the juvenile justice system into a comprehensive, more coordinated system. The subcommittee recommended that OJJDP create and support structures for meaningful youth voice and engagement at the federal, state, and local levels. The subcommittee also recommended that the President, the Congress, and OJJDP increase opportunities for collaboration on youth engagement between OJJDP and other youth-focused agencies and strengthen youth voice and engagement at the federal and state levels through legislation.

The Youth Justice and Schools Subcommittee addressed the critical need to bring the school discipline issues of expulsion, suspension, and disengagement to the forefront for policymakers and the public. As a result of zero tolerance and other discipline policies, school discipline problems are increasingly being handled by law enforcement. This has significantly increased suspensions and expulsions and has resulted in criminalizing some behaviors that, in the past, may have been considered youthful indiscretions. Consequently, some punished youth are at a greater risk of advancing from the juvenile justice to the criminal justice system. The subcommittee focused its recommendations on two issues: (1) the urgent need to make school engagement (e.g., keeping youth in school and out of jail) a major component of any juvenile justice reform effort and (2) the equally critical need to make research findings on school discipline readily available to practitioners and policymakers in practical, user-friendly formats.

The Youth Justice and Disproportionate Minority Contact (DMC) Subcommittee concentrated on ways to further U.S. Department of Justice efforts to identify and reduce disproportionality in the juvenile justice and related systems. Recognizing that a juvenile's first contact with the juvenile justice system is often with law enforcement, the subcommittee stressed the need to train all law enforcement personnel, including school-based officers, on dealing with minority youth. The subcommittee also noted that disparate racial outcomes exist in other youth-serving agencies, such as child welfare and schools. Because many community leaders, citizens, and families are unfamiliar with the DMC issue, they are not involved in DMC reduction efforts. Based on these concerns, the subcommittee's recommendations addressed the need for law enforcement training, the need to focus on efforts to reduce racial disparities in other youth-serving entities, and strategies to increase community and family awareness and understanding of the harmful consequences of DMC.

Introduction

The Federal Advisory Committee on Juvenile Justice (FACJJ) is a consultative body established by the Juvenile Justice and Delinquency Prevention Act (section 223) and supported by the Office of Juvenile Justice and Delinquency Prevention (OJJDP) within the U.S. Department of Justice, Office of Justice Programs. The FACJJ is composed of appointed representatives of the nation's State Advisory Groups (SAGs) and advises the President and the Congress on juvenile justice, evaluates the progress and accomplishments of juvenile justice activities and projects, and advises the OJJDP Administrator on the work of OJJDP. (SAGs are appointed by the Governors and assist their states in developing and implementing juvenile justice plans that their states are required to submit to OJJDP every 3 years in order to receive Formula Grant funds.)

Previous FACJJs included 56 members representing the 50 states, the District of Columbia, and the 5 U.S. territories. OJJDP restructured the advisory committee in 2011, making it smaller so that it could become more effective and efficient in advising OJJDP. The current FACJJ is composed of 14 primary members and 14 alternate members representing an array of disciplines and diverse geographic areas. At the first meeting of the restructured FACJJ in October 2011, the new FACJJ members discussed a wide variety of juvenile justice issues to identify key areas for which recommendations could be made to OJJDP, the President, and the Congress. Based on these substantive discussions, the FACJJ members established four subcommittees:

- The Subcommittee on Evidence-Based Youth Justice Practices.
- The Subcommittee on Youth Engagement.
- The Subcommittee on Youth Justice and Schools.
- The Subcommittee on Youth Justice and Disproportionate Minority Contact.

In addition to conducting their own research and review, FACJJ members made suggestions for the Annual Request for Information, which OJJDP sends to all SAGs, state juvenile justice specialists, and state disproportionate minority contact coordinators. Subcommittee members took responses to the questionnaire into account in preparing their recommendations.

Subcommittee members spent many hours on conference calls and e-mails developing recommendations and vetted the recommendations through the full FACJJ during several Webinars and two in-person meetings. After thoughtful discussion, the full FACJJ approved the 16 final recommendations presented in this report at its public meeting on December 9, 2013.

Recommendations

Primary FACJJ Recommendation

Although the bulk of this report is focused on recommendations developed by the subcommittees and approved by the full Federal Advisory Committee on Juvenile Justice, the FACJJ could not leave unaddressed the need for action related to reauthorization of the Juvenile Justice and Delinquency Prevention Act (JJDPA), including affirmation of the important role that the Office of Juvenile Justice and Delinquency Prevention (OJJDP) can play in providing leadership on critical juvenile justice issues and supporting investments in funding to promote effective practice.

Since it was established in 1974 through the JJDPA, OJJDP has served as the federal focal point for the juvenile justice system. Through the establishment of core protections for juveniles, support for research and knowledge dissemination, development of national standards, distribution of funding, and provision of training and technical assistance, OJJDP has been at the center of juvenile justice reform in the United States. Unfortunately, reductions in appropriations, constraints to budgetary control, and a failure to reauthorize the JJDPA have all combined to undermine the Office's leadership role. Because reauthorization of the JJDPA is critical to addressing the many juvenile justice issues facing the nation, including those discussed in this report, the FACJJ makes the following primary and overarching recommendation to the President and the Congress:

1. **The FACJJ strongly recommends that the President and the Congress reauthorize the Juvenile Justice and Delinquency Prevention Act, substantially increase OJJDP's funding levels, and restore the Office's budget flexibility to enable OJJDP to fulfill its critical national mission of working to prevent and control juvenile delinquency, improve the juvenile justice system, and protect children.**

Evidence-Based Youth Justice Practices

The Evidence-Based Youth Justice Practices Subcommittee developed recommendations for the full FACJJ's consideration related to the study, dissemination, and effective implementation of youth justice-focused programs, policies, and practices.

The subcommittee's use of the acronym EBPs refers to both evidence-based programs and evidence-based practices. Those practices that focus on risk, criminogenic need, responsivity, and quality implementation can be systematically implemented to increase the likelihood of positive outcomes.

Given the breadth and depth of issues surrounding EBPs, the subcommittee initially struggled with how to make its recommendations. It was important to get a solid understanding of what OJJDP is mandated to do and its views on EBPs. OJJDP must maintain the capacity to evaluate and disseminate implementable research to the field, and with that in mind, the subcommittee's recommendations reflect a consensus to focus on outcomes, particularly the measurement of positive outcomes for youth in the system.

Jurisdictions need help to bridge the gap between research and practice. Much research goes unused because it is not always clear how to use it or there are insufficient supports to use it meaningfully within the existing system. The subcommittee noted that system reform is needed and that alignment and quality improvement initiatives, based on best practices, could go a long way to help jurisdictions in their reform efforts.

The subcommittee encourages the integration of EBPs into the larger framework that views youth, the community, and those affected by crime as equally important customers of the juvenile justice system. Because this is an evolving field, it is crucial that OJJDP understand and stay current with that research and disseminate it in a useful way to practitioners. Because youth live in multiple domains, it is essential to integrate juvenile justice efforts with those of other systems that serve youth and families, including health and education.

The subcommittee engaged in significant discussions around positive outcomes before examining how much of that research translates into practical work in the field. The subcommittee deemed it equally important to identify incentives and roles for OJJDP to develop a consistent framework for action. Furthermore, it is important that researchers and OJJDP articulate intermediate outcomes and learn to incorporate them into future practice.

To address the many issues related to EBPs and to focus on positive outcomes, the subcommittee identified what OJJDP is already measuring. The team reviewed selected literature and white papers, provided specific questions for questionnaires, and examined the 3-year juvenile delinquency prevention plans that states submitted to OJJDP to determine whether individual states and local jurisdictions are trying to measure any particular outcomes related to EBPs. Information gleaned from the questionnaires and literature revealed that few states have measures they routinely, robustly track and fewer still have the capacity or desire to track the outcomes required. The subcommittee noted, however, that it may be unaware of what some jurisdictions are tracking.

The subcommittee noted the need for capacity building and providing enough information so practitioners can meaningfully modify programs where appropriate and apply lessons learned about effective components of their own best practices. OJJDP can influence the field regarding EBPs through general policy leadership and by providing funding, technical training, and assistance; focusing on research-to-practice initiatives; and serving as a clearinghouse for best-practices research and information.

Approved by Full FACJJ: Recommendations 2, 3, 4, 5, and 6

2. **The FACJJ recommends that OJJDP support efforts to identify common outcomes that can be used to assess the effectiveness of programs and practices—in particular, those outcomes that include positive youth development and prosocial skill development—in reducing "negative" behaviors.**

    a. OJJDP should host a summit with experts and selected practitioners to develop a limited number of positive youth outcomes that can be integrated into further evidence-based practices research, initiatives, and implementation strategies.

    b. OJJDP should consider additional ways that both positive youth outcome measures and EBPs (not solely programs) can be incorporated into grant solicitations, monitoring, and reporting. This presumes that there will be an ever-increasing partnership between OJJDP and grantees in "give and take" that helps inform OJJDP and the juvenile justice field as to what works best to both prevent offending and to intervene successfully with youthful offenders.

    c. OJJDP should consider the use of a limited number of national outcome measures in all of its solicitations, contracts, and training related to OJJDP's vision of "Rare, Fair, and Beneficial" to create meaningful measures of positive outcomes in the Office's activities, rather than a simplistic approach to recidivism reduction. (OJJDP envisions a nation where children are healthy, educated, and free from violence. If they come into contact with the juvenile justice system, that contact should be rare, fair, and beneficial.)

3. **The FACJJ recommends that OJJDP assess current best-practice strategies for implementing EBPs systemwide and promote the development of new strategies.**

    a. OJJDP should provide resources (publications, training, technical assistance, and funding) that can assist jurisdictions in aligning resources and practices at all levels of contact with youth to be consistent with research about what works with youth and families.

b. OJJDP should provide guidance to practitioners to minimize the loss of efficacy inherent in inadequate investment in factors such as high-quality and highly trained staff, attention to responsivity factors inherent in a relationship between adults and youth, and development and implementation of ongoing quality assurance measures to evaluate success.

c. OJJDP should continue to support research into evidence-based programs and meta-analytical research that identifies the characteristics of what works well with youthful offenders. Both specific program models and more comprehensive research into core principles and components will continue to move the juvenile justice field forward.

4. **The FACJJ recommends that OJJDP continue to emphasize juvenile justice practices that are based on solid scientific research and evidence, including programs that are listed on registries, such as the *OJJDP Model Programs Guide, Blueprints for Healthy Youth Development*, and other programs that effectively and comprehensively incorporate evidence-based practices. Furthermore, OJJDP should continue to fund studies of juvenile justice practices and programs that have not yet been conclusively evaluated.**

a. Special consideration should be given to researching practices and interactions between service providers and youth/families that are not easily captured and researched in a program model.

b. Significant interaction—often greater interaction—with youth occurs outside the confines of specific program models, yet evidence-based programs often fail to incorporate these important interactions as part of a comprehensive supervision/intervention plan.

5. **The FACJJ recommends that OJJDP continue to collaborate with other federal agencies, national organizations, and others that are focused on the needs of youth (e.g., mental health, education, behavioral health, and alcohol and other drug abuse) and that are also working to identify and develop evidence-based policies and practices that respond to those areas of need. Youth in the juvenile justice system most often demonstrate cross-system needs, yet practitioners in various systems too often operate under different frameworks and use different vocabularies.**

6. **The FACJJ recommends that OJJDP take special note of racial disparities that exist throughout the juvenile justice system and place greater emphasis on supporting evidence-based practices that can reduce those disparities.**

Youth Engagement

The Youth Engagement Subcommittee, composed of four young adults who are SAG and FACJJ youth members, recognizes that engaging young people—especially those with direct experience in the juvenile justice system—is a powerful and efficient way to improve the system. The subcommittee developed its recommendations after:

- Receiving input from youth, including those with direct experience in the juvenile justice system who attended the Coalition for Juvenile Justice's 2013 Youth Summit.

- Interviewing experts in the field who specialize in youth engagement, youth voice, and positive youth development.

- Reviewing reports and recommendations addressing youth and family voice in juvenile justice.

The subcommittee referenced the Youth Engagement Continuum, used by several youth-serving organizations, as a framework for its discussions. The continuum covers the spectrum from manipulation to full youth-initiated, shared decisionmaking and includes the following:

- **Manipulation,** in which young people are used to support causes but are given no chance to provide inspiration.

- **Decoration,** in which youth are paraded or used to bolster a cause without being directly involved in any part of the cause.

- **Tokenism,** in which youth appear to have a voice but, in reality, have no say about their participation. For example, they may sit on a board or advisory committee but have no real input into the conversation—they are just there to fill a seat.

- **Assigned but informed,** in which youth are assigned to a specific task and told precisely how to do the task and what to say.

- **Consulted and informed,** in which youth are consulted about their views but their suggestions are not taken into account or implemented.

- **Adult-initiated and shared decisionmaking,** in which a youth project is initiated by a seasoned individual—often an adult or mature young person—with the decision-making shared between the youth/emerging leader and the seasoned individual.

- **Youth-initiated and directed,** in which youth initiate and direct a project or program with an adult in an advisory role.

- **Youth-initiated, shared decisionmaking,** in which projects or programs are initiated by empowered youth who share decisionmaking with seasoned or established professionals.

The subcommittee focused on youth voice and engagement in the juvenile justice system and the importance of having youth with current or prior juvenile justice system experience involved in shaping the policies and practices of this system at the federal, state, and local levels. Subcommittee members cited powerful examples of fundamental impacts on the system as a result of youth being involved in decisionmaking at all levels. OJJDP has the opportunity to further elevate youth voice and engagement as a principle and practice across the country by modeling and supporting positive, effective, intentional, and systematic youth engagement. These recommendations are designed to transform the juvenile justice system into a comprehensive, systematic approach where youth are viewed as partners in their own path through the system and in improving the juvenile justice system.

Approved by Full FACJJ: Recommendations 7, 8, 9, and 10

7.   **The FACJJ recommends that OJJDP create consistent and well-supported structures for meaningful youth voice and engagement at the federal level on juvenile justice system issues to ensure that the voices of young people are heard on a regular, ongoing basis by government leaders and throughout the juvenile justice field.**

    a. OJJDP should establish and support a committee composed entirely of young people both with and without juvenile justice system involvement—or identify and partner with an existing body that meets these requirements—to provide insight and recommendations to OJJDP on juvenile justice programs, policies, issues, and reforms. This entity should be composed of young people representing SAGs; youth in custody; and national, state, and local juvenile justice policy, advocacy, and direct service organizations. Young adults participating on this committee should be provided with dedicated support from OJJDP and/or external organizations—including travel assistance, financial stipends, and recognition of service as deemed appropriate— to ensure that barriers to their participation do not exist and that their participation enables them to advance both personally and professionally.

    b. OJJDP should develop an intra-agency Youth and Family Engagement Team— comprising OJJDP senior staff from each division and led by the OJJDP

Administrator—that convenes at least quarterly and liaises meaningfully and coordinates with the youth committee. This team should:

- Enlist the support of representatives from other federal agencies with experience in building effective youth voice and engagement structures, experts in the field, family members of system-involved youth, and young people to create a plan for agency- and systemwide youth voice and engagement, so that OJJDP can serve as a model in this arena to states and jurisdictions.

- Include at least two Youth Justice Fellows—young people with prior or current juvenile justice system involvement—who are funded to work at OJJDP on youth voice and engagement in the juvenile justice system.

- Identify and create opportunities for youth voice and engagement within OJJDP and in partnership with other federal agencies.

c. The proposed OJJDP-supported youth committee, the proposed intra-agency Youth and Family Engagement Team, and the proposed OJJDP Youth Justice Fellows should collaborate and work in partnership with SAGs, juvenile justice nonprofits, and private foundations to build greater youth voice and engagement within OJJDP's existing work and to launch new federal and state initiatives specifically focused on youth voice and engagement. The committee should create a National Youth Speakers Bureau to provide youth who have prior system involvement with the tools, support, and a platform for sharing their stories and advice with audiences across the country.

d. The subcommittee recommended a number of other activities to OJJDP to encourage youth engagement:

- Create a national network of young people, especially young people with prior juvenile justice system involvement, to serve as training and technical assistance providers.

- Host an annual national summit on juvenile justice youth voice and engagement similar to OJJDP's annual Tribal Youth Summit, organized and led by youth.

- Ensure that OJJDP's requests for proposals require applicants to describe how their agencies or entities incorporate youth leadership and youth engagement in their activities.

- Create a national resource for youth and parents that provides advice and guidance on preventing involvement in the juvenile justice system and navigating through it.

- Incorporate youth perspectives in existing OJJDP publications and other dissemination activities.

8. **The FACJJ recommends that OJJDP support states and local jurisdictions in developing structures and mechanisms to increase meaningful youth voice and engagement on juvenile justice issues, and in transforming policies and practices to view juvenile justice system-involved young people as partners in the juvenile justice system.**

   a. OJJDP, in partnership with young people, should develop and disseminate information and resources to support states, SAGs, community organizations, and local jurisdictions in implementing policies, programs, and practices that support greater youth engagement and youth voice in the juvenile justice system.

   b. OJJDP should support states and local jurisdictions in adopting policies and practices grounded in positive youth development and strengths-based approaches that ensure that young people in the juvenile justice system are viewed as system partners.

   c. OJJDP should disseminate information on successful existing youth voice and engagement strategies at the state and local levels and should support SAGs in modeling youth engagement at the state level. OJJDP should develop a biennial report evaluating youth and family engagement nationally to determine best practices and disseminate it as a resource. OJJDP should encourage SAGs to establish committees composed entirely of youth and to appoint at least one youth ombudsman and one youth member who is currently in custody to participate in SAG meetings and activities.

   d. OJJDP should work to build capacity and resources to carry out the work of the proposed interagency Youth and Family Engagement Team and provide support in expanding youth and family engagement trainings and technical assistance at the federal, state, and local levels.

   e. OJJDP should require that the 3-year plan for each SAG include youth-led projects. Mentoring by an experienced SAG member should not be discouraged. The youth-led project(s) should be substantially completed by youth SAG members and reported on as required of all other funded activities.

9. **The FACJJ recommends that the President, Congress, and OJJDP increase opportunities for collaboration between OJJDP and other youth-focused federal agencies on youth voice and engagement.**

a. The OJJDP Administrator should work with partner federal agencies via the Coordinating Council on Juvenile Justice and Delinquency Prevention (Coordinating Council) to create a national youth leader advisory group composed of young adults who are leaders within youth-serving systems to guide these agencies and the federal government on how better to engage youth in shaping federal youth-focused policies and programs and support state, local, and tribal governments in doing so.

b. OJJDP should research current policies, practices, and structures within other federal youth-serving systems that pertain to youth voice and youth engagement to identify successful approaches from other systems that could be applied within juvenile justice.

c. The President and the Congress should amend 42 U.S.C. 5616 (section 206 of the JJDPA), Coordinating Council on Juvenile Justice and Delinquency Prevention, to include a provision for a total of three youth representatives to be appointed to the Coordinating Council by the Speaker of the House of Representatives (one), the majority leader of the Senate (one), and the President (one).

d. OJJDP should encourage the Coordinating Council to make it a priority to financially support the travel of youth representatives and appropriate adult supervisors (e.g., guardians, parents, SAG members), specifically for hotel and flight costs, to ensure their participation in the Coordinating Council face-to-face meetings to obtain meaningful engagement from the youth representatives.

10. **The FACJJ recommends that the President and Congress amend the JJDPA to include language that strengthens youth voice and engagement at the federal and state levels.**

a. Amend 42 U.S.C. 5633 (section 233) to require that at least one-fifth of each SAG be composed of young adult members, defined as individuals younger than 28, at least two of whom must have current or prior juvenile justice system involvement. Provisions should be included that outline SAG reporting requirements on young adult membership, further define what constitutes youth engagement (such as meetings attended, votes cast, and subcommittee participation), and describe how young adult members transition on their SAGs to become adult members.

b. Amend the JJDPA section on the FACJJ to require that at least one-fifth of the FACJJ be composed of young adult members, defined as individuals younger than 28, at least two of whom must have current or prior juvenile justice system involvement. Provisions should be included that outline FACJJ reporting requirements on young adult membership, further define what constitutes youth engagement (such as meetings attended, votes cast, and subcommittee participation), and describe how young adult members transition on the FACJJ to become adult members.

Youth Justice and Schools

The Youth Justice and Schools Subcommittee focused on the critical need to bring the school discipline issues of expulsion, suspension, and disengagement to the forefront for policymakers and the public. As school systems across the country have implemented zero tolerance and other punishment policies, school discipline problems are increasingly being handled by law enforcement rather than schools. This change has significantly increased suspensions and expulsions and has resulted in criminalizing some behaviors that, in the past, may have been considered youthful indiscretions and were handled by schools and parents. As a result, some punished youth are at greater risk of advancing from the juvenile justice to the criminal justice system, thus becoming enmeshed in the school-to-prison pipeline. The subcommittee recognizes that considerable research has been done on how to keep youth engaged and schools safe, but this work needs to be highlighted and presented in user-friendly formats.

The subcommittee worked hard to intentionally focus on only two recommendations for full consideration by the FACJJ. The first is broad and nonprescriptive, and the second is specific and highly prescriptive.

Nonprescriptive. If a single juvenile delinquency prevention issue must be highlighted, it is how to keep youth in school and out of jail. School engagement should be front and center of any juvenile justice reform at all levels: federal, state, and local. OJJDP can lead this effort by ensuring that the issue of school exclusion versus school engagement is addressed when discussing or implementing any juvenile justice reform effort.

Highly prescriptive. Although research on school engagement exists, the findings are not readily available to practitioners and policymakers in practical, user-friendly formats. Many subcommittee members who have worked with juvenile justice agency personnel, school administrators, school boards, and other stakeholders note that these individuals are not likely to read voluminous reports. Instead, an abridged document is needed that can serve as a roadmap, is straightforward, and includes tangible steps for implementing the best school discipline policies and practices. Such a document would provide snapshots of policy issues that the public, educators, and policymakers should consider when their school districts begin to reform their disciplinary approaches. The document should spell out policies that answer specific questions, such as, "If a student is excluded from school, where will he or she go?" Should that student be kept out of school for 1 day, 2 days, 5 days, or some other length of time? Does the school offer the student alternative programming? Such a document should be brief—perhaps 5 pages, not 55 pages.

Recent work by the U.S. Department of Education through the Supportive School Discipline Initiative provides resources, best practices, and legal guidance on school discipline for schools and educators. Also, the Council of State Governments (CSG) is developing a comprehensive school discipline document, due out in the coming months, that may guide OJJDP work in this area.

The subcommittee has been following the work of the CSG and desires to champion the work being done to develop a consensus in the area of school discipline. However, because the subcommittee is concerned that the consensus effort may not fully embrace well-researched steps, members strongly suggest that a more practical roadmap is needed for school officials to use when school discipline comes under review.

The subcommittee also feels strongly that its suggestions and any eventual work done on them should not be linked to the requirement for new money, thereby reducing concerns from juvenile justice agencies or school districts that these suggestions are unfunded mandates. Rather, the subcommittee is recommending the serious next steps needed to effect attitude and policy changes in the area of school engagement that can be taken without the need for federal assistance.

Approved by Full FACJJ: Recommendations 11 and 12

11. **The FACJJ recommends to Congress, OJJDP, and other relevant federal agencies that the issue of school engagement should be highlighted as a key item in juvenile justice reform.**

The FACJJ recognizes the work that is being done in the area of juvenile justice reform and the reinvestment of federal, state, and local dollars to more effective incarceration, intervention, and prevention strategies. At the same time, the FACJJ believes special attention should be given to school engagement because research repeatedly confirms that the school-to-prison pipeline is real, and any reform effort must substantially raise the importance of school engagement.

12. **The FACJJ recommends that OJJDP be actively involved in the development and dissemination of a roadmap for schools to consider when revising or reforming school discipline policies.**

The FACJJ recognizes the ongoing work of the CSG (and others) and the U.S. Department of Education, and the support given by OJJDP and the foundations, to identify and promote "good" versus "bad" discipline policies within the school environment. Considerable research on the topic has been done, but the FACJJ strongly feels that one or more straightforward, practical documents must be developed to help schools implement best practices on issues of school discipline.

Youth Justice and Disproportionate Minority Contact

The Youth Justice and Disproportionate Minority Contact Subcommittee concentrated on ways to further U.S. Department of Justice (DOJ) efforts to identify and reduce disproportionality in the juvenile justice and related systems. The subcommittee noted the need to identify local efforts and best practices that have demonstrated success in decreasing DMC and that can facilitate other innovative practices to reduce DMC. The subcommittee's recommendations address the need for law enforcement training and the need to focus on reducing racial disparities in other youth-serving entities (e.g., child welfare agencies and schools) and on increasing family and community understanding about DMC.

Recognizing that a juvenile's first contact with the juvenile justice system is often with law enforcement, the subcommittee stressed the need for law enforcement training on dealing with minority youth. The subcommittee believes that every recruit, seasoned officer, commander, and others within law enforcement agencies in the United States should participate in mandatory training on how to deal with youth. OJJDP's DMC Reduction Model specifically identifies training and technical assistance on cultural competency within youth and staffing practices as an important way to reduce DMC. The arrest point has considerable impact as a gateway leading to disproportionality throughout the justice system contact points, including referral, diversion, detention, petitioned/charges filed, delinquent findings, probation, confinement in secure correctional facilities, and transfer to adult court. If implemented, the recommended OJJDP-approved trainings have the potential to greatly reduce DMC across these other points of contact. Training should include frontline supervisory support in the field and should be adopted as a culture within all justice system agencies. OJJDP also should include training for school-based officers, especially in light of research indicating that the school-to-prison pipeline increases DMC considerably at this arrest point.

The subcommittee also noted that it would be helpful if DOJ required grant proposals to include information on how a proposed project would reduce DMC. Law enforcement needs a concise indicator or assessment tool or protocol, produced in collaboration with OJJDP, to help ensure that these agencies' DOJ-funded projects, as appropriate, are helping to reduce DMC.

The subcommittee expressed concern about racial disparities within multiple systems (e.g., child welfare and schools) and their impact on DMC and youth who interact across these systems. Funding is needed for pilot programs that research confirms have been able to bring systems together to identify best practices and achieve positive outcomes for youth in multiple systems.

Finally, based on conversations in the field, it is apparent to the subcommittee that families and communities need to be educated about DMC. It is a consensus across the states that awareness of DMC too often exists in its own isolated community, namely, the people who are working in the field or those who are somewhat familiar with DMC initiatives. Individuals in other roles who can significantly impact DMC at critical contact points are not sufficiently aware of or actively engaged in reducing disparities, or it may not take priority over other issues they face. It is important to support DMC coordinators and others working to address disparities, so they can reach the larger population of service providers who can also address DMC-reduction efforts. Community programs that serve system-involved youth may be able to align their goals; infuse best-practice models within programming; and make it a priority to educate their constituents, fellow service providers, and families.

Approved by Full FACJJ: Recommendations 13, 14, 15, and 16

13. **The FACJJ recommends that OJJDP collaborate with other relevant federal agencies to develop training for school-based officers and educators on efforts to address the school-to-prison pipeline and its impact on DMC in the juvenile justice system.**

14. **The FACJJ recommends that DOJ include, in all of its law enforcement requests for grant proposals, language that requires grant applicants to indicate how they are addressing juvenile DMC in their communities and how the proposed grant activity will promote those efforts.**

15. **The FACJJ recommends that OJJDP encourage and support study and research on disparities within multiple youth-serving systems and their impact on juvenile DMC. OJJDP should use the research to develop models or best practices for cross-systems collaboration to reduce DMC in the juvenile justice system.**

16. **The FACJJ recommends that OJJDP support an initiative to fund and create a campaign that educates families and communities about DMC, its impact, what is being done to address the issue, and how they can be part of the solution.**